DK READERS

Level 2

Dinosaur Dinners
Fire Fighter!
Bugs! Bugs! Bugs!
Slinky, Scaly Snakes!
Animal Hospital
The Little Ballerina
Munching, Crunching, Sniffing,
   and Snooping
The Secret Life of Trees
Winking, Blinking, Wiggling,
   and Waggling
Astronaut: Living in Space
Twisters!
Holiday! Celebration Days
   around the World
The Story of Pocahontas
Horse Show
Survivors: The Night the
   Titanic Sank

Eruption! The Story of
   Volcanoes
The Story of Columbus
Journey of a Humpback Whale
Amazing Buildings
Feathers, Flippers, and Feet
Outback Adventure: Australian
   Vacation
LEGO: Castle Under Attack
LEGO: Rocket Rescue
¡Insectos! en español
Ice Skating Stars
MLB: A Batboy's Day
MLB: Let's Go to the Ballpark
Star Wars: Journey through Space
¡Bomberos! en español
Sniffles, Sneezes, Hiccups,
   and Coughs

Level 3

Spacebusters: The Race to
   the Moon
Beastly Tales
Shark Attack!
Titanic
Invaders from Outer Space
Movie Magic
Plants Bite Back!
Time Traveler
Bermuda Triangle
Tiger Tales
Aladdin
Heidi
Zeppelin: The Age of the Airship
Spies
Terror on the Amazon
Disasters at Sea
The Story of Anne Frank
Abraham Lincoln: Lawyer,
   Leader, Legend

George Washington: Soldier,
   Hero, President
Extreme Sports
Spiders' Secrets
The Big Dinosaur Dig
Space Heroes: Amazing Astronauts
The Story of Chocolate
LEGO: Mission to the Arctic
NFL: Super Bowl Heroes
NFL: Peyton Manning
NFL: Whiz Kid Quarterbacks
MLB: Home Run Heroes: Big
   Mac, Sammy, and Junior
MLB: Roberto Clemente
MLB: Roberto Clemente en español
MLB: World Series Heroes
MLB: Record Breakers
MLB: Down to the Wire:
   Baseball's Great Pennant Races
Star Wars: Star Pilot

A Note to Parents and Teachers

DK Readers is a compelling program for beginning readers, designed in conjunction with leading literacy experts, including Dr. Linda Gambrell, Director of the Eugene T. Moore School of Education, Clemson University, and past president of the National Reading Conference.

Beautiful illustrations and superb full-color photographs combine with engaging, easy-to-read stories to offer a fresh approach to each subject in the series. Each DK READER is guaranteed to capture a child's interest while developing his or her reading skills, general knowledge, and love of reading.

The five levels of DK READERS are aimed at different reading abilities, enabling you to choose the books that are exactly right for your children:

Pre-Level 1 – Learning to read
Level 1 – Beginning to read
Level 2 – Beginning to read alone
Level 3 – Reading alone
Level 4 – Proficient readers

The "normal" age at which a child begins to read can be anywhere from three to eight years old, so these levels are only a general guideline.

No matter which level you select, you can be sure that you are helping your child learn to read, then read to learn!

LONDON, NEW YORK, MUNICH,
MELBOURNE, AND DELHI

Editor Elizabeth Hester
Senior Designer Tai Blanche
Assistant Managing Art Editor
Michelle Baxter
Publishing Director Beth Sutinis
Creative Director Tina Vaughan
DTP Designer Milos Orlovic
Production Ivor Parker

Reading Consultant
Linda Gambrell, Ph.D.

Produced by
Shoreline Publishing Group LLC
President James Buckley, Jr.
Art Director Tom Carling
Carling Design, Inc.

Produced in partnership and licensed by
Major League Baseball Properties, Inc.
Vice President of Publishing
and MLB Photos: Don Hintze

First American Edition, 2005
05 06 07 08 09 10 9 8 7 6 5 4 3 2 1
Published in the United States by DK Publishing, Inc.
375 Hudson St., New York, NY 10014

A catalog record is available from the Library of Congress.

ISBN 0-7566-1209-8 (Paperback) 0-7566-1208-X (Hardcover)

Color reproduction by Colourscan, Singapore
Printed and bound in China by L. Rex Printing Co., Ltd.

Photography credits:
All photographs by Michael Burr, except for the following:
AP/Wide World: 27; Getty/MLB Photos: 5, 26; L.A. Dodgers: 23

*Thanks to the Los Angeles Dodgers for their kind cooperation in
producing this book. Thanks to Conor, Travis, and Mark for their
help. And very special thanks to Michael, Matthew, and Kelly for
sharing their day at the ballpark!*

Discover more at
www.dk.com

 READERS

BEGINNING TO READ ALONE 2

Let's Go to the
Ballpark

Written by James Buckley, Jr.

DK Publishing, Inc.

It is a bright, sunny day.
Matt and Kelly are excited.
Today they are going on
a special trip.
They are going to a Major
League Baseball game!

Matt and Kelly are big
baseball fans.
They love to
play baseball
with Dad
in the park
and watch
games on
television.

Dodger Stadium

But they have never been to a
game in person.

Today, Dad is taking them to see
the Los Angeles Dodgers play at
Dodger Stadium.

Let's go with them to the ballpark!

Their first stop is the ticket booth.
Dad buys three blue tickets.
Blue is the Dodgers' team color.

Each ticket has a seat number on
it. Some seats are close to the field.
Others are high above it.

Matt, Kelly, and Dad join a big
crowd of people walking toward
the stadium entrance.

Famous ticket
Fans save their
ticket stubs as
souvenirs. This ticket was from a famous
World Series victory by the Dodgers in 1988.

A stadium worker takes the tickets.
He tears them in half and gives
the stubs back to Matt and Kelly.
Matt and Kelly click through the
turnstiles and go inside.

The seats are starting to fill
with people.
Matt and Kelly look at their tickets
and try to find their seats.
There are hundreds of seats.

Matt and Kelly look out over
the crowd.
They are amazed at all the people!

The stadium seats rise above the playing field.

The Dodgers' old home

This usher's cap was used in Ebbets Field in Brooklyn, New York. The Dodgers played there from 1912 to 1957.

Matt and Kelly ask an usher to help find their seats. The usher wears a stadium uniform so people will know she is here to help.

She leads Matt and Kelly down a long flight of stairs. She stops at Row M.

"You have seats 9, 10, and 11," she says with a smile.

"Thank you," says Matt. "Go Dodgers!"

After the family finds the right
seats, it's time to find lunch!
At the ballpark, fans can pick from
many tasty treats.
Matt, Kelly, and Dad stop at a
stand to buy something to eat.

Matt and Kelly choose hot dogs.
Dad buys a soda and a bag
of popcorn to share.

After lunch, they discover that the
ballpark is a great place for dessert!
"Peanuts!" yells one vendor.
"Ice cream!" shouts another.

*Fans can buy snacks
from vendors like
this one.*

On the way back to their seats,
the family stops at a souvenir stand.
They join a crowd of kids and other
fans looking at all the choices.

"Wow," says Kelly. "Look at
this cool shirt!"
Kelly picks out a blue Dodgers shirt.

Then she helps Matt pick out
a keepsake for himself.

"Dad, can I get some baseball cards?" asks Matt.

"Sure, Matt," Dad says. "I hope you get some of your favorite players!"

Kelly, Matt, and Dad return
to their seats.
The teams are lined up on the field.
Now all the fans are standing.
Dad explains that it's time to
sing the National
Anthem.

Before every
Major League
game, fans
and players
honor America by singing
"Oh say can you see . . ."

Kelly, Matt, and Dad stand up, too.
They look at the American flags
flying high above the ballpark.
The flags flap in the wind.
They look bright against the
clear blue sky.

Then the umpire calls out,
"Play ball!" and the game begins!

Matt and Kelly cheer for their favorite team.
Today, the Dodgers are playing the Pittsburgh Pirates.

The two fans look out at the field.
The grass has a pattern of stripes, made with a special lawnmower.

The white baselines are bright against the brown dirt base paths.
The Dodgers' home uniforms are bright white, too.

From the seats, the fans can see all the action.

Matt and Kelly look around
the ballpark.

Above the outfield is a scoreboard.

The lights of the scoreboard show
the score of the game.

It also shows which player is at bat.

By the fifth inning, the Dodgers
are ahead 5–2!

Fans in the stands can also keep track of the score.

They draw symbols and numbers on a special score sheet.

The score sheets help remind them of the plays they saw in the game.

Dad shows Matt how to mark his own scorebook.

Keeping score with Dad

At a game, you never know when a foul ball might come your way. In the sixth inning, a ball flies right to Matt!
Kelly and Dad help catch it.

Kelly likes to watch the batters for ideas on how to be a better hitter on her own team.

The Dodgers' young outfielder Jayson Werth steps up to the plate.

A home-run swing!

Kelly watches him carefully.

She watches Jayson swing. Then she jumps to her feet to cheer—it's a home run! Jayson scores a run for the Dodgers!

People all around
Matt and Kelly cheer
for Jayson, too.

They make lots
of noise.
There are 50,000
people at Dodger
Stadium today.

Kelly wears her
Dodgers hat and shirt. But some
fans wear no shirts at all.
Instead, they paint big blue letters
on their chests.
The letters spell D-O-D-G-E-R-S!

Other fans carry signs that help
them root for the Dodgers.
Fans also wear jerseys with the
names and numbers of their
favorite players on the back.

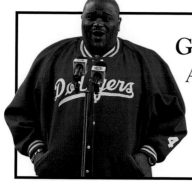

God Bless America
At many ballparks, stars like Ruben Studdard help lead the fans in seventh-inning songs.

After the Pirates make their last out of the seventh inning, everyone stands up again.
Matt and Kelly look around.
Why is everyone standing up now?

Then they hear the announcer: "Fans, it's time for the seventh-inning stretch!"

The music starts and everyone sings "Take Me Out to the Ballgame."

This baseball tradition has been around for nearly 100 years. Matt, Kelly, and Dad try to sing louder than anyone else!

In the bottom of the seventh
inning, the Dodgers score again!
Now they are ahead 7–4.

Kelly and Dad do a high-five,
just like the players.
What an exciting game!

Finally, it is the ninth inning.

Everyone gets to their feet when there are two outs.

Just one more, and the Dodgers will win.

A Pirates batter hits a long fly ball.

Shawn Green of the Dodgers catches it for the final out.

The Dodgers win!

Outside the ballpark, Matt and Kelly cool off in a spray of water.

Cooling off on a hot day

Now it is time to go.

The three fans have had a great time at the ballpark.

They watched a good game.

They munched on hot dogs and snacks.

They even got a chance to sing!

They have some souvenirs to take home, too.

"Did you have a good time?" Dad asks Matt and Kelly.

"You bet we did, Dad," Kelly says. "And I'm glad the Dodgers won!"

Matt has just one more question:
"When can we go again?"

Baseball Songs

Matt and Kelly sang two songs at the game they attended. The National Anthem is sung before the game. "Take Me Out to the Ballgame" is sung between the top and bottom of the seventh inning. Here are the words to these two famous songs so you can sing along at the ballpark!

The Star-Spangled Banner (National Anthem)

Written by Francis Scott Key, 1814

Oh say can you see, by the dawn's early light,
What so proudly we hailed at the twilight's last gleaming?
Whose broad stripes and bright stars, through the perilous fight,
O'er the ramparts we watched, were so gallantly streaming?
And the rockets' red glare, the bombs bursting in air,
Gave proof through the night that our flag was still there.
Oh say, does that star-spangled banner yet wave
O'er the land of the free and the home of the brave?

Take Me Out to the Ballgame

Written by Jack Norworth and Albert Von Tilzer, 1908

Take me out to the ballgame.
Take me out with the crowd.
Buy me some peanuts and Cracker Jack.
I don't care if I ever get back.
So it's root, root, root for the home team.
If they don't win it's a shame.
For it's one, two, three strikes you're out,
At the old ball game!

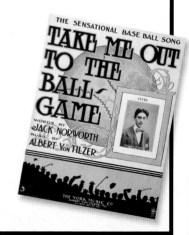

Index

ballpark workers 8,
   10, 13
Brooklyn, New York 10

catching foul ball 22

Dodger Stadium 5, 24

Ebbets Field 10

fans 9, 19, 24–25

Green, Shawn 29

home run 23

K sign 21

Los Angeles Dodgers
   5, 14, 19, 20, 23,
   24–25, 28–30

National Anthem 16

Pittsburgh Pirates 19, 29

scoreboard 20
scorekeeping 21, 28
seventh-inning
   stretch 26-27
stars 26
souvenirs 14–15

"Take Me Out to the
   Ballgame" 26
ticket booth 7

umpire 17

vendors 13

Werth, Jayson 23
World Series 7

DK READERS

My name is

_____

I have read this book

Date

_____